MW01291213

LARGER THAN OURSELVES

THE EARLY BEGINNINGS OF THE JESUS PEOPLE

DUANE PEDERSON

with Mark Dixon

Foreword by Steve Gottry

THE HOLLYWOOD FREE PAPER

2014

Published by
THE HOLLYWOOD FREE PAPER
A voice of the Jesus People since 1969

Post Office Box 1949
Hollywood, CA 90078-1949
duane@hollywoodfreepaper.org
http://www.hollywoodfreepaper.org/

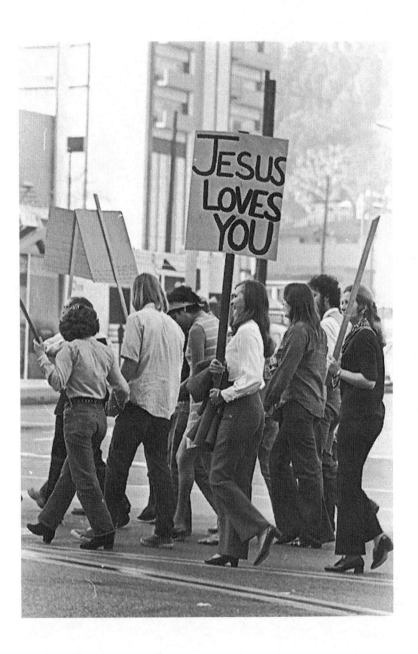

FOREWORD

Have you ever watched a magician perform a magic trick, and then you immediately wondered, "How did he do that?"

Way back in 1964 in rural Minnesota, I met a young magician. I watched him perform on several occasions, and every time I was mystified. "How did he do that?"

Of course, I knew his act wasn't really magic. These weren't really miracles. I knew God had nothing to do with it. I knew it was all an illusion.

I kept in touch with the young magician continuously over the following years.

In early 1970, I boarded a plane in Minnesota to visit my friend. He was no longer a magician. He was living in Hollywood, California, and was involved in some sort of "movement." He and his friends occupied three or four small houses on Fountain Avenue, near Hollywood and Vine.

Most were people in their teens and twenties, most of them longhaired and unshaven, and most of them dressed in "Goodwill reject" clothing. They reminded me of the "counterculture" crowd of the time. I expected them to be busy making signs protesting the

Vietnam War. I expected them to be angry, unhappy, and wasted on the chemicals that others of their (and my) generation were trying.

Instead, they were happy. No, more than that, they were joyful! They spent their days and nights laughing, singing, and praying. They invested their time telling other young people who were searching for life's meaning about the meaning they had found... about the reason for their joy. They were proclaiming Jesus Christ as their Lord and Savior. Not in a heavy-handed way—but in a loving, caring, gentle way.

In phone calls, my friend had told me about these young men and women before I went to visit him. He called them "Jesus People." I thought he might be joking—except I knew him better than that.

I quickly realized that these Jesus People were not a magic trick. They were not an illusion. They were not even the result of something my friend had done. They were a miracle, because God had everything to do with it.

I recall thinking to myself, I wonder if there are any more of them, or if this is it.

The answer to that question was quick to follow, because the next night my friend invited me to the Hollywood Palladium for a "Jesus People Gathering."

The moment we walked in, I was confronted by more than 4,000 glowing faces and loving hearts—Jesus People who had come together to love and worship God, and praise the name of His Son. "There really are more of them," I thought.

I listened to musicians who were new to me play amazing music and talk about their faith. I'll never forget them—especially a young talented singer-songwriter named Larry Norman. I was so moved by his music that I bought all of his albums and CDs, and still listen to them on my iPod today.

When the music died down and they all became quiet, my friend got up on the stage and told the crowd what being a "Jesus Person" really means. Hundreds throughout the audience made the life-shaking decision to follow Christ that night. The next day, many of them gathered at the Santa Monica Pier, where they shared in Holy Communion and humbly and obediently followed in the next step of faith—and were publicly baptized by my friend, Duane Pederson.

That was virtually my only experience with the Jesus People Movement until I read this book.

Now that I know the full story, I realize the scope of the miracle that was unfolding right before my eyes. The multitudes were being fed, and clothed, and healed, and loved. Jesus was being proclaimed. And no one was seeking glory or demanding credit—least of all, my friend Duane. They were just doing what God had asked them to do.

Fast-forward more than 40 years. Duane Pederson is still my friend. He is still doing what God has asked him to do—simply "love the unloved."

I pray this miraculous story touches you as deeply as it touched me. But the best is yet to come, because Jesus is still on the Throne!

Steve Gottry
Mesa, Arizona

PREFACE

Some true stories don't translate well into motion pictures or television. They're too improbable, the coincidences too far-fetched, no one would believe that such things could actually happen in real life. The early beginnings of the Jesus People Movement is one of those true stories.

It began with God speaking. Not once, but many times. He spoke to a beatnik sailmaker in San Francisco who heard God's voice on the Oakland Bay Bridge. He spoke to a long-haired, bearded hippie mystic and seeker who would later play a key role in launching two new Christian denominations. He spoke to an Iowa farm girl who had worked with dangerous street gangs on the mean streets of Brooklyn. And he spoke to a magician and stage performer who was haunted by the blank expressions and empty eyes of the street people he encountered on Hollywood Boulevard.

The movement arose spontaneously in several cities up and down the west coast, with people who at first didn't even know each other. This is proof to me that it was initiated by the Holy Spirit of God, and not by us. The movement began like the strike of a match in the hearts and minds of young people in each of those cities, long before any word reached them that what they were experiencing was also happening elsewhere at the same time. The genesis of the Jesus People Movement was clearly of supernatural origin, and not by the hand of man.

Duane Pederson
Los Angeles, California

I
SAN FRANCISCO

1
URBAN RENEWAL

It was 1956 when bulldozers coughed diesel smoke into the placid San Francisco morning air and crawled forward to demolish the first of 2,500 Victorian homes in the city's sprawling Western Addition. Sixty square blocks of a thriving African-American community would eventually be labeled as blighted by the Redevelopment Agency, and whole neighborhoods of family homes, barber shops and grocery stores would be leveled in the name of urban renewal. Popular jazz clubs like Leola King's Birdcage and Blue Mirror disappeared, along with hundreds of other black-owned businesses. Despite repeated promises from city government, most of the displaced families were never allowed to return.

By 1960, a young crowd of free spirits, beatniks and students from San Francisco State College, mostly white and in their twenties, had filtered into the ravaged neighborhood, settling particularly in the Fillmore District. They started an assortment of small communes and co-ops in older homes that had escaped the bulldozers, and named them after their streets. The Fulton Street People occupied a turreted Queen Anne Victorian house on Fulton west of Divisadero; there were the Central Street House, the 857 Divisadero House, the

O'Farrell Street House, and more. There were student crash pads, peacenik communes, folksinger co-ops and drug-user flats.

The O'Farrell Street House was a ramshackle Victorian row house on the south side of O'Farrell run by a Zen Buddhist beatnik, and was home to a number of notable Beats. It had a "mythical aura about it ... very intense, very Beat, an older group." Neighborhood teens knew the House as a source of fresh green peyote buttons from a mail-order cactus nursery in Laredo, Texas, which one of the commune's occupants kept in a paper grocery bag under his bed and freely gave away.

One young couple at the O'Farrell Street House was Ted and Liz Wise, then in their mid-twenties. Ted, who had grown up in California's gold rush country, had married Liz while in college, and had just returned from a four-year hitch in the U.S. Navy during which he learned the craft of sailmaking from the ship's boatswain. After Ted's discharge from the Navy, he and Liz had followed their "beatnik sentiments" to San Francisco.

2
FASTEST GAME IN THE WEST

In July 1961, the Wise's first child, a daughter, was born, and the young family moved just across the Golden Gate to the picturesque enclave of Sausalito, bordering the sheltered waters of Richardson Bay with postcard views of Angel and Belvedere Islands. During World War II, Sausalito was home to bustling shipyards, and the Navy christened a Tacoma-class frigate the USS Sausalito in 1943 to honor the city's industrial contributions to the war effort. In the postwar years the former shipyards were abandoned, and a colorful houseboat and recreational boating community had developed in their place, affording Ted the opportunity to ply his trade of sailmaking for the many yachts and sailboats that called Sausalito's lively waterfront home.

The Wises soon had a second child, a son, and the couple settled into the bohemian culture of their new community. Their circle of friends included artists, poets and jazz musicians, yachtsmen and other sailors, yogis, Buddhists, Communists and anarchists. Ted Wise would later describe the eclectic social sphere of Sausalito in the 1960s as "the fastest game in the west."

Viewed from San Francisco Bay, much of American society in

the postwar years had become numbingly staid and conformist. When World War II ended, the thousands of women who effectively ran the nation's defense plants and other industries during the war and were widely caricatured as "Rosie the Riveter" returned to roles of wife and mother, while men home from the battlefield took over as the family breadwinner.

Comfort and consumerism became national values, and the unquestioned acceptance of traditional roles and mores was celebrated in popular television shows like "Father Knows Best." The beatnik, who not only didn't fit into mainstream society but didn't want to, was stereotyped by the young Bob Denver's goateed slacker, Maynard G. Krebs, in the TV sitcom "The Many Loves of Dobie Gillis."

Like many who came of age during or immediately following the Korean War, Ted and Liz Wise found themselves feeling alienated from what they saw as a homogenized, white-bread lifestyle and were drawn to the countercultural, drafty-garret existence of the bohemians and beatniks and, by the early 1960s, the incipient hippie culture. Disillusioned, the Wises and their growing tribe of unconventional friends increasingly saw themselves as members of an interstitial or gap generation, having literally fallen through the cracks of postwar middle-class society. "Many of our adventures together," Ted would later relate, "were mixed with large doses of LSD."

3
HE IS BACK

It was during this period that Ted had an epiphany of sorts while driving home from Berkeley late one night across the Oakland Bay Bridge. His later account of those few minutes was surreal, but he was certain of one thing: he had experienced the voice of God.

Ted had been taking his first tentative steps toward becoming a follower of Jesus, but was still struggling with exactly what that meant in his life. He had decided that sharing his decision with their friends in Berkeley would be an important step. Ted and Liz each took a hit of LSD before driving to Berkeley. They arrived to find their friends all high on marijuana, but nevertheless Ted told the group about his spiritual decision. The cold, awkward silence that followed made the couple uncomfortable, and they soon left and started back to San Francisco.

Ted would later describe an almost out-of-body experience on the bridge. His senses told him he had stopped the car and was walking, but at the same time he knew he was continuing to drive across the bridge. Frightened and confused, he prayed, and began to hear what he was sure was the voice of God guiding him safely across the bridge and giving him a command. "You must speak My words to everyone," the voice instructed him. "You are to say, 'He is back.' Nothing more."

Liz, suffering an equally difficult if less dramatic disturbance of her own "spiritual ecology," began attending the rather conservative First Baptist Church of Mill Valley, then pastored by John MacDonald, in search of her childhood spiritual roots and as a positive influence for the couple's two children. Ted would later quip that Liz was hoping to "run into her long lost spiritual Friend, Jesus."

The Wises' Sausalito flat was crowded day and night with friends and friends-of-friends sharing their food and other material goods and, as more and more of them did indeed find Jesus, they freely shared Him with each other as well. This very natural, almost organic way of sharing their possessions and their faith would become one of the marks of the Jesus People.

4
OUT OF THE QUESTION

A curious renaissance was brewing across the bay in San Francisco, a budding hippie culture that echoed the changes taking place a continent away in New York City's Greenwich Village. The epicenter of the movement was a neighborhood below Golden Gate Park where two streets named for early San Francisco pioneers Henry Haight and Munroe Ashbury crossed. Ted and Liz Wise moved freely through this strange new Eden among old friends and new acquaintances, sensing both the physical and spiritual needs of the constantly-evolving community, and later discussing them with the other members of their growing tribe in the already overpopulated Sausalito apartment. At the same time, they gradually began to introduce Liz's pastor, John MacDonald, to the life of Haight-Ashbury.

A radical communal group of hippies called the Diggers were living and working in the Haight, providing free "crash pads" (temporary lodging) for many of the homeless youth who continually wandered the streets, as well as free food (including whole wheat bread baked in coffee cans that became a Digger trademark), free tie-dyed clothing, and more, from a rented storefront. Their activities had the aura of street theater, as when they served a meat-and-vegetable stew in Golden Gate Park through a huge yellow picture frame that they called their Free Frame of Reference. From catch-us-if-you-can Free Stores (a forerunner of today's thrift shops) to the Haight's first Free Clinic, everything the Diggers offered was free for the asking.

When the Health Department condemned the Diggers' building, Ted asked John MacDonald to let them use a room at his Mill Valley church. "I want to show these Diggers that church people do care about them," Ted explained. "I want to know, is the church willing to help in a time of need like this?" To Wise, this was a showdown: he had laid his cards on the poker table, and was 'calling' the longtime Southern Baptist pastor to show his hand.

"To say yes was out of the question," MacDonald would later insist. "But to say no bluntly could also turn away forever from the organized church what appeared to me to be a growing opportunity to meet the spiritual need of a group of young people." These opposing thoughts collided in his mind with trepidation about bringing the request before his Board of Deacons back in affluent, suburban Marin County, and the pastor was able to offer Wise only "what must have been a pitiful stammer."

LIVING OUT THE BOOK OF ACTS

As concerned as Ted was about the Diggers, a more pressing crisis demanded his attention — the Wises had been evicted from their Sausalito apartment. The flat had been full to overflowing with friends and guests, with hippies coming and going at all hours. Sleeping bags and their occupants littered the floors in every room, and eviction was predictable, if not inevitable. Ted knew he could find accommodations for his own family, but the endless stream of young people who had depended on the Wises' flat as a safe harbor "now became objects of Ted's prayer and concern."

Dan Sands, whom the Wises had befriended while attending Sierra College in Auburn, had taken courses on communal life at the Free University of San Francisco. As the men discussed their options, the idea of a Christian commune began to take shape, and Dan and his wife Sandy soon joined the Wises and two other couples (Jim and Judy Doop, and Steve and Sandi Heefner) to create an experimental Christian commune. The group rented a large, rambling two-story farmhouse in the rural village of Novato in northern Marin county, about 20 miles north of Sausalito and a half-hour's drive from the Haight-Ashbury district across the Golden Gate. Initially they just called it the Big House.

Within a month or so a young artist from southern California, Lonnie Frisbee, joined the commune. A talented painter, he had received a scholarship to San Francisco's prestigious Academy of Art, the "art school of art schools" near Golden Gate University in the city's Financial District. Jim Doop described him initially as "all hair with a handsome face and a smile and laugh that charmed everyone. His voice was strong and ... there was an appealing resonance when he spoke." Lonnie had encountered Ted and Liz Wise while exploring Haight-Ashbury, and was intrigued enough by their plans to join them in Novato.

An old sea captain and recent convert named Jack Shaw christened the commune the House of Acts, because the four couples and Lonnie "agreed on one thing: we ought to live out the Book of Acts like a script." Lonnie painted the new name on a sign to make it official.

"We began to sell our possessions — houses, cars — and to call nothing our own," Ted would later explain, "then we proceeded to offer our hospitality to as many others as we had room for." Soon the familiar multitudes of sleeping bags began to appear across the Novato ranch house floor, out the door and onto the porch, and "the openness of the House of Acts to all comers was practically without limit."

It was the legendary Summer of Love, and the spiritual awakening that would soon become known as the Jesus People Movement had begun.

THE LIVING ROOM

With the loss of the Diggers' makeshift headquarters, the denizens of Haight-Ashbury had to get by without the aid the group had so merrily provided. At the same time, hippie life in the Haight was being glamorized to the rest of America by the mainstream media. As a result, a deluge of literally thousands of teenagers and college students was pouring in, but the neighborhood's already stressed infrastructure could not accommodate the influx of people and the situation quickly deteriorated.

By this time, the district was "crowded with youngsters — lonely, hungry and, above all, caught in frightening circumstances and needing assurance of friendship." The need for a new presence in the district to reach out to its burgeoning sidewalk infantry was never far from Ted's mind.

At Ted's urging, John MacDonald and a handful of other local pastors "provided some of the means and all the respectability" the House of Acts family needed to rent a storefront in the Armenian Rosdom Hall on Page Street between Ashbury and Masonic. The long narrow space was just a block from the panhandle of Golden Gate Park where the legendary "be-ins" were taking place. It would prove to be an advantageous venue for the new outreach.

The room was sparsely furnished in "early Salvation Army" style, suitable for relaxed conversations over a bowl of soup, and the one-on-one, person-to-person style of ministry Ted and his friends preferred. "If someone came along who had no other place to sleep, quite naturally he was invited to spend the night there." Its name reflected the same feeling of congenial hospitality: the Living Room.

Letters in psychedelic colors formed the shape of an ox yoke in the front window, spelling out the words of Jesus from Luke 23:34, "Father, forgive them, for they know not what they do." Other scripture verses adorned the interior walls in a similar flowing style. Donuts, coffee and often soup were freely shared with visitors who came in off the street to learn more about Jesus or just to talk about their own lives.

Each day the Living Room crew made the half-hour drive from Novato across the Golden Gate bridge to San Francisco in a 1954 Plymouth coupe they had been given by a member of the First Baptist Church of San Francisco. They wandered through the communal houses and crash pads of Haight-Ashbury as though always among friends, sharing the news of Jesus with everyone they met.

ISAIAH'S GRANDSON

In his first few months at the House of Acts, it became clear to everyone that Lonnie Frisbee, the bohemian painter who had come to San Francisco to attend the Academy of Art, was not a stereotypical art student. Genial and outgoing with shoulder-length hair, a full beard and bright eyes, Lonnie could radiate a commanding presence that has been described as "the charisma of Jim Morrison flowing from the mantle of an Old Testament prophet." The description wasn't far off. He wore a hooded tunic similar to those worn by St. Francis of Assisi in medieval paintings, and once jokingly described himself as looking like Isaiah's grandson.

Lonnie's housemates learned that he was a seeker and mystic. He described visions from God he had experienced while experimenting with LSD with friends in Tahquitz Canyon in the summer of 1967, near the desert city of Palm Springs in southern California. During one such adventure, he painted a life-size image of Jesus on the rock walls of the canyon, and saw a vision of himself baptizing huge crowds of young people in the ocean as hundreds more watched from the beach and the cliffs above. Lonnie believed that God had told him he would be given a unique ministry as an evangelist. On another trip to the desert oasis, Lonnie baptized each of his friends at Tahquitz Falls.

At one point, Lonnie told his housemates in Novato about a young woman named Connie Brewer whom he had met at the Brotherhood of Eternal Love, a mystical commune in Silverado Canyon above Laguna Beach in Southern California reputedly connected with guru and former Harvard professor, Timothy Leary. Members of the commune sought spiritual experiences through psychedelics including LSD, as well as religious traditions from Hinduism to Mahayana Buddhism to Christianity. Lonnie decided to hitchhike back to Orange County to find Connie. He invited her to join him in Novato, where they were married in April 1968.

Before long, Lonnie again hitchhiked to southern California, this time as an itinerant evangelist. An unexpected encounter along the way would change Lonnie's life, and begin a new chapter in the Jesus People Movement.

8
THE BEAN FIELDS

Coastal morning fog chilled endless acres of lima beans on the flatlands of Costa Mesa as the pale sun revealed the outline of the San Joaquin Hills to the east. Swedish immigrant Carl Johan Segerstrom and his wife Berthe had settled in Orange County in 1898, starting a family farm where they raised dairy cattle, alfalfa and lima beans. Segerstrom and his sons farmed their rich land with horses, and later with yellow Caterpillar tractors. For half a century the family had grown lima beans in Costa Mesa, with as many as 2,100 acres of beans under cultivation. They became one of the largest growers of lima beans in the United States.

In 1950, Caltrans, the State's transportation agency and builder of the region's iconic freeways, connected Los Angeles with Costa Mesa and Santa Ana via an extension of Interstate 5 they christened the Santa Ana Freeway. White-collar executives in downtown Los Angeles saw the opportunity to live in the picturesque and still semi-rural environs of Orange County while continuing to work in L.A., and the land rush to Costa Mesa and points south was on.

By the mid-1960s, Costa Mesa was booming and Henry Segerstrom, Carl and Berthe's grandson, had begun to develop portions of the family's suddenly valuable farmland as housing and business ventures. Recognizing a shift in Americans' shopping patterns to indoor malls housing multiple stores in one air-conditioned location, the enterprise, now known as C.J. Segerstrom and Sons, embarked on an ambitious project: an upscale mall in the flatlands of Costa Mesa. The shopping center was launched as South Coast Plaza, anchored by two major department stores, May Company and Sears. Established local merchants along Newport Boulevard like Reed's Te Winkle Hardware and Crawford's Pharmacy found themselves fighting a losing battle to lure shoppers back to the city's once-bustling downtown strip.

Barely half a mile north of Crawford's Pharmacy, another losing battle was being fought. A tiny cottage church called Calvary Chapel had dwindled to a mere 25 members and was on the brink of financial collapse. In a final bid to stave off ruin, the little church boldly called on the middle-aged pastor of a flourishing interdenominational church across the Trabuco hills in Corona, and asked him to come to Costa Mesa and lead Calvary Chapel.

Chuck Smith had already left behind a 17-year career in the International Church of the Foursquare Gospel, a Pentecostal denomination, hoping to "reach a broader cross-section of people" at Corona Christian Center, and he felt his ministry there was just starting to bear fruit. The congregation in Costa Mesa, by contrast, was discouraged and thinking about closing. Nevertheless, Smith and his wife Kay visited a Sunday service at the small white cottage on Church Street, and subsequently agreed to make the move.

The tiny congregation began to thrive under Smith's leadership, and the cottage at the corner of Church and Walnut Streets was soon overcrowded. Several temporary relocations later, during which the congregation continued to grow, Calvary obtained the former Greenville School site adjacent to the Segerstroms' remaining lima bean acreage. A persistent urban legend continues to this day that

Calvary Chapel "started in the middle of a bean field."

9

YOU'LL BLOW THEIR MINDS

It was around this time that the Smiths' attention was drawn to the many beatniks and hippies in the beach communities of Orange County. The couple visited the local beaches frequently, and often found themselves talking about the hippies as they drove home. Chuck's reaction was, "Why don't they get a bath, get a job and get a life?" Kay was more sympathetic: "You know, they are so desperately in need of Jesus." Chuck didn't think they were reachable.

While attending the University of California at Irvine, the Smiths' daughter Jan began dating a young man named John Nicholson who was also at UCI. Nicholson had briefly dabbled in the counterculture in Haight-Ashbury and had experimented with LSD. One day when he was at the Smiths' home, Chuck and Kay said, "John, we want to meet a hippie. You know, a real honest-to-goodness hippie."

Not long after, John was driving on Fairview Drive near Orange Coast College in Costa Mesa when he spotted a young hippie hitchhiking. Remembering Chuck and Kay's curious request, John stopped to give him a ride. The boy who climbed into John's car "had flowers in his hair and bells on his cuffs and looked a lot like some of the pictures of Jesus."

"I want you to come over and meet some friends of mine," John told him. "You'll blow their minds."

When Chuck opened the door, standing on the porch next to John was a young man in a tunic with long dark hair and a full beard, bright eyes and a warm, engaging smile. John said, "Chuck, I want you to meet Lonnie Frisbee."

"I wasn't prepared for the love that came forth from this kid," Chuck would later recall. "His love for Jesus Christ was infectious, the anointing of the Spirit was on his life, so we invited Lonnie to stay with us for a few days."

Lonnie moved in and began to bring friends, and soon the house was full. "Honey, this isn't going to work," Chuck told Kay. "We're not ready for a hippie pad." The Smiths rented a two-bedroom house on 19th Street, not far from the little white cottage on Church Street where Calvary Chapel had started. Chuck recruited a friend, John Higgins, Sr., to move in with Lonnie, and the house ministry (one of the first "Jesus Houses" in southern California) was christened the House of Miracles. The community grew rapidly: 21 young people were living at the house by the end of the first week, and 35 by the end of the second. Bunk beds were soon installed in the garage, and "one kid was even sleeping in the bathtub," Chuck would later recall.

As rapidly as hippies and surfers entered the House of Miracles, a steady stream of enthusiastic young Jesus freaks from the house began moving out to evangelize in Costa Mesa and beyond. One group, perhaps inspired by Lonnie's tales of his earlier adventures, headed for Tahquitz Canyon to witness to the young people who were drawn to the desert oasis in search of a spiritual experience.

The House of Miracles would later grow to include 19 communal Jesus Houses, and would eventually become the basis of John Higgins' Shiloh Youth Revival Centers, which became a string of more than 100 Christian communal houses across North America.

By then, Connie had traveled south and joined Lonnie in Orange County. Lonnie quickly became a crowd-drawing youth evangelist at Calvary Chapel Costa Mesa, filling the Wednesday night Bible studies to capacity, witnessing to surfers and other young people at nearby beaches during the day and inviting them to Smith's church for the nightly services.

Some of the older members of Calvary Chapel were not happy with the sudden influx of young hippies and surfers. They complained that the young people's bare feet were staining the expensive carpet in the sanctuary, and the dirty clothes of some of the hippies had soiled the upholstered pews. The complaints led to a tense confrontation between Chuck Smith and the church's Board of Deacons, where Smith offered a simple solution. Rip up the carpet and have concrete floors, he told the Board. Take out the upholstered pews and have plain wooden benches. But the kids stay.

10
BY WATER AND THE WORD

One brilliant summer afternoon, a baptism like no other was held at Little Corona Beach, a crescent of shell-strewn white sand at the foot of Ocean Boulevard between the Newport Bay jetty and Crystal Cove, south of Corona del Mar State Park. A hundred or more young Jesus People scrambled up the rocks to the eel-grass-covered cliffs overlooking the beach.

The teenagers and young adults awaiting baptism on the sand below took a few tentative steps toward the water's edge. Guitars began to softly play as the "cloud of witnesses" lining the cliffs linked arms and joined in harmony on popular praise choruses, swaying to the gentle rhythm as they sang. In a home movie made of the baptisms, the white sails of a catamaran passed by just offshore as the summer sky gave way to a postcard-perfect orange and pink sunset.

Chuck Smith, with thinning hair dripping and a joyful smile, took the hand of a recent convert and led her out into the shimmering water, protected by the beach's natural reefs from the pounding surf beyond. It was a beach literally made for baptisms. Nearby, Lonnie Frisbee, waist-deep in the clear Pacific waters, spoke quietly to another young convert before baptizing him in the name of the Father and the Son and the Holy Spirit.

Looking back across the gentle swells to the others waiting on the beach and the hundreds of onlookers that lined the cliffs above, Lonnie would later say he realized that this was the moment God had promised him in his vision at Tahquitz Falls.

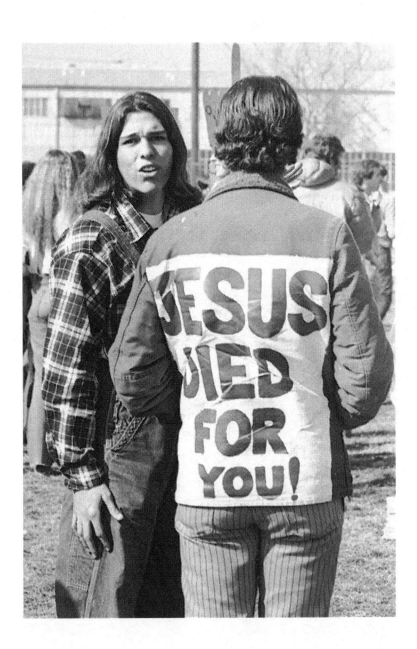

II

SEATTLE

11
METAMORPHOSIS

A six-hundred-foot steel and concrete tower rises above the Lower Queen Anne neighborhood of downtown Seattle, between the blue expanses of Lake Union and Elliott Bay. Its once-futuristic shape remains a distinctive feature of the city's skyline. The revolving "flying saucer" crown with observation deck and restaurant has turned for half a century at the leisurely speed of one rotation every 47 minutes. The Space Needle was built for the 1962 World's Fair, and stands as an ironic reminder of the Emerald City's high-flying growth years.

At the end of World War II, Seattle embarked upon an unprecedented period of economic prosperity, fueled by lucrative aerospace contracts for the city's largest employer. "Boeing was hiring," one observer would later recall, "and the economy was booming." It would boom for the next twenty-five years.

Beginning in the late 1950s, Seattle in general, and the neighborhood surrounding the University of Washington campus in particular, became one of the focal points for the emergence of the Sixties youth culture in the Pacific Northwest. The transformation began with the Beats and "fringies" (local slang for almost any nonconformist youth) and continued with the hippies and flower children, and eventually the Jesus Freaks.

Throughout the early- to mid-1960s, these idealistic young dropouts and free spirits found their way to the university neighborhood or "U District," and an eclectic mix of little shops and venues catering to their bohemian tastes began to appear. This was particularly true along University Way NE, known to natives as the "Ave," the area's main thoroughfare that was beginning to emit a cautiously countercultural vibe. If Haight-Ashbury was becoming the Greenwich Village of the west coast, the U District was becoming the Haight-Ashbury of the Pacific Northwest.

Almost without warning, the hip neighborhood abruptly blossomed into living color. The Pamir House featured folk-singing in a former private residence at 41st Street and the Ave, and the Eigerwand Kaffeehaus a block or two north specialized in "rancid coffee and fiery conversation," both staples of the beatnik diet. Grad student Steve Herold transformed the moribund Id Bookstore into a vibrant oasis, and another grad student, Paul Dorpat, teamed up with radical activist Walt Crowley to publish Seattle's first underground newspaper, the *Helix*. A group of UW students had launched an Experimental College which continues at the university to this day.

By the "Summer of Love" in 1967, UW students were going to the Pamir House or the Eigerwand, "playing chess in the window and sipping some of that funny strong coffee from San Francisco and being intellectual." The neighborhood's metamorphosis into Seattle's psychedelic and countercultural haven was complete, but another wave of change was gathering energy just offshore and would soon break with the force of a tsunami.

12
AN ARMY FOR JESUS

The striking young woman with long auburn hair and intense eyes who appeared in the U District one bright Seattle day looked nothing like an army recruiter. The street kids or "Ave rats" who wandered University Way NE certainly looked nothing like soldiers. But a recruiter she was, and many of Seattle's aimless youth were about to become her troops.

Linda Meissner had served in the tough urban slums of New York City with evangelist David Wilkerson, author of "The Cross and the Switchblade," in the early days of his Teen Challenge ministry which began as an outreach to street gangs and heroin addicts. Working side-by-side with Wilkerson out of a large two-story Georgian brick residence in the Clinton Hill neighborhood of Brooklyn, she ventured deep into dangerous gang territory to meet with girls and young women trapped in lives of violence and addiction.

Linda had been raised a Methodist in the tiny rural town of Montezuma, Iowa, and attended Central Bible College, a conservative Pentecostal school in Springfield, MO known for preparing its students for pastoral ministry or the mission field. But nothing could have prepared the quiet farm girl for the wretched atmosphere of "death on the installment plan" she encountered on the desperate streets and alleys of New York. "You can actually feel the presence of evil," she wrote in a letter home to her family. "I know that my life is in danger. I have only one desire — to burn out for God."

It was during her service with Teen Challenge that Meissner believed God was telling her to return to Seattle, where she had previously worked as part of Wilkerson's Teen Harvesters in 1965, and she experienced a vision of herself leading an army of teenagers marching for Jesus. Arriving there in late 1968, she immediately began recruiting street kids from the Ave and young people from across the city for what would become her Jesus People Army.

13

ON THE VERGE OF REVIVAL

Barely eleven miles inland from Puget Sound, the rural village of Cathcart lies in a buffer zone between the pumpkin farms and stallion stables of the Snohomish River valley and the rapidly vanishing timberland beyond. Woodsy and sparsely populated, it seemed an odd locale for a Pentecostal revival, but as young travelers Jim Palosaari and Sue Cowper drove up in their decorated hippie van with macrame curtains, right before their eyes was an honest-to-goodness revival tent set up in the middle of the Washington woods.

A local pastor, Ruben Korpi, had imported Russell Griggs, a Canadian evangelist in a three-piece suit, to preach in the remote location for a week. At the meeting that evening, Jim and Sue were the only ones who 'got saved.' When the crusade folded the following night, Griggs took the newly minted converts to a coffeehouse he had heard about on 2nd Avenue in downtown Seattle. There, Sue would later recall, they met a "petite, fiery, unstoppable, formidable woman" who shared her vision of "a vast army of devoted followers of Christ that would sweep the world with the message of the Gospel in the last days." The woman was Linda Meissner.

Linda wasted no time drafting the new arrivals for her campaign. Sue would later remember being "out on the dark street witnessing to a pack of Hell's Angels" soon after they arrived. Seattle was "just on the verge of revival," and Linda and her crew were ramping up quickly for it. "Once in town, Linda shared her vision of an army of God wherever she could."

Recruits found Meissner's style "less trippy and more demanding," movement historian Jon Trott would later observe. "She wanted disciples, not just converts, as her extensive training programs and communal houses attested." Her arguably more serious approach appealed to those "who were aching to commit to something real, total and lasting."

Working with Griggs, who began setting up an outpost of the Jesus People Army just across the Canadian border in Vancouver, Linda's early efforts were aimed mostly at getting the word out and recruiting. She started a local radio program called "Youth Speaks," a coffeehouse called Youth-o-Rama, and told her story at coffeehouses, churches and any other venues that were open to her. As their numbers grew, the JPA began publishing an underground newspaper called *Agape*, advertising Jesus People events and meeting places as we would soon begin doing in the *Hollywood Free Paper* in Los Angeles. The JPA opened a coffeehouse called the Catacombs near the Space Needle downtown, complete with a house band, Glorious Liberty. A drop-in counseling center called the Ark that also served as Meissner's informal office was added.

A pair of communal Jesus Houses, the House of Caleb and House of Esther, opened in the Wallingford district of Seattle's North End, an area thrown into chaos by the prolonged construction of Interstate 5 that had split the neighborhood in half. By November 1969, two more houses in Seattle, the House of David and House of Zacchaeus, were formed, as well as Emmanuel Farm in Sumas, WA and the men's House of Joshua commune in Edmonds, WA.

Later, the Eleventh Hour, a ministry to Seattle's street youth similar in concept to the Living Room in Haight-Ashbury, opened in a rented storefront at 1st and Madison near the waterfront in downtown Seattle.

Twenty miles south in the hamlet of Auburn, WA, the Seattle JPA held an organizing meeting at Green River Community College. Excitement was high, and the onstage band played to a packed house. Thomas Simms, a local pastor, offered his basement as an initial meeting place for an Auburn JPA. The venue quickly became known as the Rap Shack. Later a storefront coffeehouse was opened on the town's main road, and some of the JPA members lived together communally in an older home southwest of downtown Auburn where they also reached out to hobos from the Northern Pacific rail yards on the edge of town.

14

ROAD WARRIORS

Soon, a road-warrior contingent of Seattle's Jesus People Army traveled to Spokane, WA for a series of outreach gatherings in the city's High Bridge Park. Laid out in the early decades of the 20th century by the designers of New York's famous Central Park, High Bridge occupies a dramatic swath of two hundred wooded acres overlooking the scenic Spokane River. By the time the Jesus People arrived, the park was a major anchor of the predominantly white "barbecues and tricycles" bedroom community of Peaceful Valley. Carl Parks, a minister with local connections and a street ministries background, helped JPA organize the series of outdoor meetings and preached.

Three members of a popular local rock band called the Wilson McKinley attended the gatherings at the park and individually had life-changing encounters with Jesus, and made a decision to join the hippie Christian community Parks was organizing called the Voice of Elijah. So certain were they of their new direction that the three band members packed their instruments into their tour van, dropped it off in the driveway of the band's fourth member, and walked away from the original Wilson McKinley forever.

Shortly thereafter, Carl Parks asked the three musicians to provide music for his street evangelism. The trio resurrected the name of their former band, and drove nonstop to Lewiston, ID, to pick up a talented bassist they knew. When they returned to Spokane, the reorganized Wilson McKinley became the house band of the Voice of Elijah.

Under Parks' leadership, the community began doing street ministry, working with Spokane's homeless, and planning road trips to destinations as far away as Colorado and Iowa. Voice of Elijah opened a coffeehouse called I Am, and began publishing a Jesus newspaper, the *Truth*. The Wilson McKinley released their first LP after their collective rebirth. Unknown to anyone in Spokane, an early edition of their newspaper and a copy of that first album were about to take a quiet road trip of their own.

15

AWESTRUCK

Squeezed onto a narrow strip of coastline by a range of mountains colorfully called the Devil's Prongs, the former salmon canneries, utilitarian homes and small workaday businesses of Kodiak, AK huddle together on the shore. A busy ferryboat, the M/V Tustumena, named for an Alaskan glacier, connects the area's scattered towns and smaller islands by sea, plying the frigid blue swells of Chiniak Bay near the top of the Aleutian chain.

One of those islands, just offshore from Kodiak, has played many roles. In two centuries it has seen whaling by the native Alutiiq, commercial ice production, a sawmill, fur trapping, a Navy wireless station, and a legacy of Christian missions that is the true spirit of tiny Woody Island.

In the late 1950s, the American Baptist Churches established a Christian summer camp on the island called Camp Woody that would be run by Baptist missionaries Norman and Joyce Smith. The Smiths had for a number of years operated a boat ministry aboard a forty-foot Navy surplus buoy tender they named the Evangel. Equipped with hymnbooks, a phonograph and folding chairs, the small but spunky vessel literally brought church to many of the rough-and-tumble fishing villages that bordered the Alaskan waters. Rev. Smith ably piloted the boat and served as its seagoing pastor. When Camp Woody opened, the Smiths continued to visit remote villages on the Evangel when the demands of the camp allowed.

As the 1960s slid into the 70s, the world-weary despair and disillusionment that permeated Greenwich Village, Haight-Ashbury and the U District in Seattle was being felt by young people in Alaska as well. The culture of "sex, drugs and rock-and-roll" had found its way up the coast to Anchorage and even Kodiak, and not just as a cynical mantra. "Nearly everyone knew someone who had died or come home wounded, psychologically or physically" from the war in Vietnam, the Smiths' then-teenage son Timothy would later recall. "The smell of weed was common wherever young people gathered on Kodiak streets, and the town's homegrown, hard-drinking ways brought their own sense of despair."

But in early 1971, the early stirrings of something new were being felt in Kodiak. A Bible study that began at the summer camp unexpectedly continued after camp through the autumn and into winter, growing from "a handful of kids who had been to Camp Woody" to more than 80, including young men from the Navy base. Students at the local high school "shrugged off lunch in favor of going to a church across the street to pray," Smith recalled. "We brought our Bibles to school, spoke openly of our faith, and took on a kind of purposeful exuberance."

Then, the news they didn't even know they were waiting for arrived. Just as the counterculture had traveled up the coast from the lower 48 to Alaska several years before, a copy of the *Truth* newspaper and a Wilson McKinley album now found their way to Kodiak from Spokane. They landed in the hands of an older Russian immigrant named Nina Gilbreath, a former missionary who shared them with the youth Bible study Timothy and his friends attended. The teens were "awestruck" to learn that what they had been experiencing locally in Kodiak was also happening simultaneously elsewhere, and there was a name for it, and for them. It was the Jesus People Movement, and they were Jesus People. Somehow it seemed to fit.

"We ordered bundles of the *Truth* papers, and a new ministry was born," Smith later recalled. "Soon every Saturday, rain or shine, freezing or soggy, we were out in front of the bars and stores of downtown Kodiak, passing out *Truth* papers to appreciative and non-appreciative alike."

16
DELICATE NEGOTIATIONS

The organization built by Linda Meissner in Seattle and Russ
Griggs in Vancouver provided a home base from which ambassadors
like Jim Palosaari and Sue Cowper could build relationships in other
communities as God gave them opportunities and the confidence to
walk into new territory. JPA outposts appeared, each with its own
unique flavor, at first nearby in Auburn, Edmonds and Everett, then
across the Cascade Range to Spokane and Yakima in the wide plateau
of the Columbia Basin, and finally outside of Washington to Boise in
western Idaho.

The road warriors reached Milwaukee, WI just as the firm
footing of JPA's Seattle-Vancouver base began to falter. Linda and
Russ had made a fateful decision to join with the Children of God, a
controversial religious sect, despite sincere efforts by Palosaari and
others to dissuade them. The Jesus People Army had not lived up to
Meissner's vision, and her followers lacked the total dedication she
believed she saw in the disciples of the COG. Linda may have seen in
the Children of God "what her Jesus People Army did not have —
numerical prosperity and disciple loyalty," a COG insider would later
remark. They would realize too late that the source of the new

group's fanatical loyalty was incompatible with the Jesus People Movement.

"We practiced a lot of deception," the COG insider, Deborah Davis, would later explain, "and people just got sucked in." Davis, the daughter of COG founder David "Moses" Berg, conducted the delicate negotiations with Meissner and Griggs, and would later admit that "the poor Jesus People Army had no idea what was going on. I know that if we had told them the whole story, they never would have joined." Only a portion of the Jesus People Army followed Linda and Russ into the COG, and in the leadership vacuum left behind in Seattle, the remaining group splintered.

Half a continent away, Jim and Sue were establishing Jesus People Milwaukee, and a vibrant, countercultural neighborhood called Brady Street was rapidly becoming their home.

17

LITTLE ITALY

Colorful neon signs flickered to life in the windows of Glorioso
Brothers' Italian grocery after another hectic day selling olive oil,
mortadella and provolone to residents of Little Italy on Milwaukee's
Lower East Side. The lofty spire of St. Hedwig's Catholic Church
dominated the sunset sky above the traffic of city buses and cars on
Brady Street as the sons of Polish and Italian immigrants returned
home from day jobs in riverside breweries and mills.

Victorian duplexes with cheerfully painted Queen Anne
stickwork lined the bustling ethnic street, their entrances perched
three or four steps above the sidewalk to accommodate the peculiar
basement apartments known locally as Polish flats. Typically rented
to students or young couples in the postwar years, these curious
downstairs dwellings, as well as the main houses above them, were
increasingly occupied by beatniks and hippies in the mid- to late-
1960s as immigrant families traded up to nicer homes in the suburbs.

Head shops, coffeehouses, thrift stores and vintage clothing
sellers appeared up and down a twelve-block stretch of East Brady
Street as the neighborhood became the vibrant nexus of Milwaukee's
counterculture. Comic-book artist Denis Kitchen started publishing

underground comics as Kitchen Sink Press. A nascent anti-war movement began to emerge.

When the road warriors from Seattle's Jesus People Army invaded Milwaukee, the Palosaaris wasted no time organizing a noisy Jesus march down one of the city's major thoroughfares to attract attention. The march ended with a rally at the county War Memorial Center, a community venue on the shore of Milwaukee Bay at the city's Veterans Park. A band called the Crimson Bridge from Chicago played what the Milwaukee Journal later called "ear splitting music." The event was most Milwaukeeans' first glimpse of these strange new Jesus freaks and their blond, bearded leader, but it wouldn't be their last.

A coffeehouse called the Jesus Christ Power House was quickly opened in a large former hardware store at Brady and Cass. A banner nearly the length of the building's front facade announced to the neighborhood Jesus' words from Acts 1:8 — "You shall receive power when the Holy Spirit comes upon you." A newspaper was launched called *Street Level*, designed to resemble Milwaukee's then-popular underground weekly, the *Kaleidoscope*. A Jesus band called Sheep was formed and they were quickly inundated with more invitations to play at schools, churches and parks than they could handle. Glenn Kaiser soon formed a second band called Charity, which would later change its name to Resurrection Band. A magazine, *Cornerstone*, was started.

The group arranged to use the former 315-bed National Convalescent Hospital at 4th and Reservoir as a headquarters and Discipleship Training Center to teach new converts the Bible and spiritual principles, a concept that would later be replicated in Hollywood and elsewhere.

18

MOVING ON

A similar revival was sweeping the Scandinavian countries as God began to move there, and the Palosaaris (Jim was a native Finn) along with the Sheep band and some of Milwaukee's older members headed for Europe.

A local pastor, J.W. Herrin, who had joined Jesus People Milwaukee along with his wife Dawn and their daughters, launched out with a new traveling team in a bright red school bus with the Resurrection Band, playing impromptu concerts in parks and churches along the way.

The team traveled across the eastern half of the United States and finally found a home at Faith Tabernacle, at Grace and Broadway in Chicago. The Chicago group would later become Jesus People USA, and the Resurrection Band and Cornerstone magazine became important components of their ministry. A Christian music festival called Cornerstone was started and continues today as part of a thriving JPUSA community still based in Chicago. *Cornerstone* magazine continued publishing until 2003.

"A large bus and several cars with Jesus painted on the side" would suddenly appear in a neighborhood, an article in a rural

Michigan newspaper said of the traveling team's arrival. "Thirty-six freaky-looking kids spill out onto the streets. Girls with ankle-length dresses and long-haired boys, fortified with armloads of papers, would scatter and start rapping with the closest passerby."

III

HOLLYWOOD

19
SLEIGHT OF HAND

Viewed from an office window in any of the multistory art deco buildings along Hollywood Boulevard, the terrazzo and brass stars that make up the Walk of Fame are not laid out in a strictly uniform pattern, rather they seem to have been casually sprinkled along the dark grey tiles of the sidewalk by some unseen hand. There are more than 2,400 of the five-pointed, coral-pink stars, enough to sustain the illusion that anyone at all might take the Greyhound to this Mecca of entertainment, be "discovered" while working for minimum wage in a car wash or waiting tables, and become the next celebrated face in the tabloids or on the silver screen.

Illusions were what first brought me to Hollywood in 1963. I was a professional comedian-magician (not a ventriloquist as has often been inaccurately reported), creating illusions each night in lounges and nightclubs, distracting the audience with nonstop comedy and snappy patter to keep them in stitches while I performed my feats of léger-de-main.

It paid the bills for several years, but I no longer imagined my name on one of those faux-marble stars, if indeed I ever had. Like the words of the song "On Broadway," when you work in show business for a living, sooner or later "the glitter rubs right off, and you're nowhere."

For a time I enjoyed performing at the Japanese Village and Deer Park, an enchanting theme park not far from Disneyland that featured pearl divers, dolphins, koi ponds and tame deer roaming free for children to pet and feed. When that show closed, I appeared in the pilot of a children's television show, "Earl the Purple Squirrel and his Tree-house Friends." Those were good times. But by the autumn of 1969, as the days grew shorter and nights in Los Angeles turned chilly, my career as an entertainer seemed to be coasting to an uncertain future.

As I walked down Hollywood Boulevard quite late on one of those chilly nights, the riot of small newspaper racks that lined the curbs of every block began to seep into my consciousness. Lurid underground newspapers, the "counterculture" press, were everywhere, preaching revolution, drugs and sex to a generation for whom the glitter had long since rubbed right off. At the intersections, jaded young people handed out the papers with a blank expression that told me they couldn't have cared less whether I read their paper or not. As each traffic light would change I walked on, but their faces, their eyes, continued to haunt me.

20
WHAT'S WRONG WITH US?

During the beatnik and early hippie eras, the street scene had been made up of musicians, artists, students, flower children and assorted dropouts, exploring altered states of consciousness, but after the Summer of Love the Sixties slid to an uncomfortable stop. Haight-Ashbury, Seattle, Hollywood and other youth magnets began to see more runaways, stumbling down their own much darker path, often filled with loneliness, nights of being rented and used, and alcohol and drugs to numb the pain.

"When I ran away the kids were into love and peace, now it's a much more desperate thing," a 20-year-old runaway from Boston declared. "Most of the kids are doing junk, just looking for a total escape. Nobody trusts anybody anymore."

God was giving me opportunities to reach out to the street people one or two at a time, but that was too slow, the problem too large. I had lived in Hollywood long enough to know that an underground street newspaper would quickly find its way into the hands of many of the runaways who had adopted Hollywood Boulevard as their surrogate home.

It may have been at the coffeehouse with my cup of hot tea, or somewhere on the Walk of Fame, feeling like just one tiny person staring up at a cold, starless sky, but somewhere that night it all came together. None of those cheap newspapers were telling people the truth. Not one. The best of them offered only temporary highs that might help you feel better for a while. The worst of them led to death, and then nothing, and none of those blank-faced kids on the corners deserved that.

As a silent prayer, the evangelist side of me said, "God, what's wrong with us Christians?"

I imagined Hollywood Boulevard lined with happy Christian young people excitedly handing out a newspaper all about Jesus. I didn't know if it had ever been tried before. I just looked back up at that starless sky and said "Jesus, if You'll give me the means with which to do it, I'll put out a newspaper telling people about You." The fact that I knew nothing about printing a newspaper didn't occur to me until later.

Several Christian businessmen I knew in the Los Angeles area contributed the funding for starting the paper, mostly on the basis that I not mention their name. The idea of a Christian alternative newspaper struck most of them as strange, and my plan to print ten thousand copies of the first issue must have sounded like lunacy, but nevertheless each wrote a check, and within a few days I had raised the amount the printer said it would cost. I had a name for it — the *Hollywood Free Paper*, a takeoff on the name of the notorious counter-culture weekly the *Los Angeles Free Press* — and that night I sat down in my small apartment and began to pull together ideas for the first edition.

21

WE LOVE YOU, CALL COLLECT

The primitive layout that began to take shape on my kitchen table was a bit sketchy on content and more than a bit rough around the edges, but the energy and fire were there. God's vision for the *HFP* was already clear: a strong lead article, several thought-provoking smaller pieces, at least one cartoon feature, a bulletin board of places and events, and a poster for your bedroom wall. I can't take credit for those ideas; I wasn't a newspaper editor then and I'm still not one today. As that first edition began to practically put itself together before my eyes, it quickly became obvious Who was in charge. And even in this tentative, unpolished form, the potential of this new medium to spark a response among the young people of Hollywood Boulevard was obvious.

The national epidemic of runaways had inspired Word Records to produce a dramatic spoken-word recording of a father's poignant letter to a runaway daughter, and the daughter's equally moving response. Writer Martin Wark scripted the conversation, setting the father's despair and angst against the teen's yearning to be independent, and Christian musician Ralph Carmichael composed appropriate music. A popular television host, Art Linkletter, and his real-life daughter Diane were selected to portray the parent and runaway child. The record was titled "We Love You, Call Collect."

Soon after the album was recorded, and just a few days before the first Hollywood Free Paper was to go to press, Diane fell to her death from her sixth-floor condo at the Shoreham Towers, a luxury high-rise in Hollywood. The belief at the time was that the incident was a drug-related suicide, possibly due to an LSD flashback, although toxicology tests by the Los Angeles coroner later showed there were no drugs in her system. The tragedy of Diane's death ironically caused sales of the album to soar. We devoted a full page of the first issue to the text of Art and Diane's dramatized father-daughter conversation.

On the campus of the University of California at Berkeley, the organization Campus Crusade for Christ had launched a project called the Christian World Liberation Front, a takeoff on the Third World Liberation Front that was pushing for ethnic studies programs at San Francisco State University and at UC Berkeley. Led by former Penn State statistics professor Jack Sparks, the Campus Crusade crew had begun publishing a newspaper called Right On, and we reprinted with permission a cartoon and a poster from one of their early issues to round out the content of the first *HFP*.

In the cartoon feature by Ray Hawkins, Jr., a young, bearded revolutionary wearing a bandolier became gradually more conservative and 'establishment' in his appearance and philosophy as the cartoon progressed, hinting at the way revolutionary movements often become cold and institutionalized over time.

"The only way to purify the system is to destroy it and start all over again," the young radical in the cartoon began. "We must unify all radical people for the accomplishment of our objective. All people must be helped to see the need for revolution." By the end of the last panel he is aged and balding in a suit and tie, talking of membership, committees, and enforcing discipline. Clearly, his revolution was over.

The featured poster was an Old West style wanted poster for Jesus, describing him as the "notorious leader of an underground liberation movement" spreading an "insidious and inflammatory message." What teenager wouldn't want to be part of that? The first issue ended with an appeal for "groovy people" to distribute the HFP. Everything was ready by the deadline, and I eagerly took the product of my night's work down to the print shop early the next morning. The printer delivered the 10,000 copies right on time.

22
I WANT TO KNOW MORE

I was already involved in street ministry on the gritty streets of downtown Hollywood, a shell of the once-bright motion picture colony whose dark alleys, then as now, were home to drug dealers, prostitutes and pimps. Some of the street people had begun to call me the pastor of Hollywood Boulevard. So it was natural for me to take a bundle or two of our new paper with me whenever I ventured out on my daily (and nightly) rounds.

To my amazement, very few of the street people refused to accept a copy when I offered them one, and I didn't see anyone throw them away. To the contrary, it thrilled me to see little groups of two or three suddenly form on the sidewalk, standing and reading the newspaper God had compelled me to publish. The 10,000 copies were soon distributed, and I felt a little let down when the last one was gone.

Up to this point, I had wondered whether anyone would actually read the *HFP*. I wondered if anyone would be affected by this very simple telling of the Gospel. I wondered if anyone would write back. I was pretty certain the answer to all those questions would be a resounding No.

A couple of days after I handed out the last copy, I was astonished to find my post office box jammed almost airtight with mail. As I began to go through the letters, I realized almost all were from street people, and they wanted to know more about the Jesus they read about in the paper. Many were written in pencil, scrawled on scraps of paper or a piece of an envelope, sometimes barely legible and poorly spelled. A few were typewritten. But all expressed the same hunger:

"If your Jesus Christ is really for real, man, I want to know more. I'd like to rap with you about the guy. Where can we meet? When? Are you gonna have another paper?"

The response was thrilling, but almost a bit intimidating. How could I answer so many letters? Some didn't even have a return address, others were signed only with a first name. A few gave their telephone number. More than a few sent in dollar bills for a "subscription" to the paper. I realized I was committed to publish another edition, and another. God seemed to be shoving me in that direction.

With the stack of opened mail spread out before me, I began to pray. I told God that if He wanted me to keep on printing the paper, I would do it, but I'd need Him to keep helping me with it, and continue providing the means. I shouldn't have been surprised when He did both, and the *Hollywood Free Paper* continued to be published in one form or another, with a few breaks and gaps in the action, until 1988.

23
AN INFLAMMATORY MESSAGE

Almost immediately and for the next several years, writers, a gifted photographer named Tom Jackson, wonderful artists and cartoonists like Dale Yancy, Warren Heard, Lance Bowen, and others, literally appeared out of the woodwork and volunteeered to help, and the Spirit moved through these talented young people to turn the *Hollywood Free Paper* into something more exciting and useful and lasting than I ever could have alone.

For several years beginning in 1969, the *HFP* had the privilege of serving as one of the main printed voices of the Jesus Movement, taking news of the Jesus People and our revolution to coffeehouses, communes, Jesus houses, and the streets of Hollywood, Minneapolis, Detroit, and Cleveland. Then somehow it went international, and news poured in from Stockholm, Oslo, Manila, Hong Kong and beyond.

During those first few years, more than 14 million copies of the *HFP* were printed and distributed around the world. 35,000 people wrote to tell us they found a personal relationship with Jesus after reading the *HFP*. 30,000 Bibles and New Testaments were given to new brothers and sisters.

God was moving in the hearts and lives of teenagers and young adults in an unusually direct and intensely personal way, and those teenagers and young adults are what became the Jesus Movement. God was making it unmistakably clear — He was doing a new thing, it was all about His Son, and no one would be turned away. It was a spontaneous and sovereign work of the Holy Spirit.

Through it all, we knew in our hearts that we weren't the ones making these exciting things happen, but Jesus Himself was. We counted ourselves blessed to have a part in it. Then we stood back and watched God turn it all into something bigger than we would have dared to imagine.

24

TILL THE GROOVES WORE OUT

Music was a major part of the movement, and local Jesus Music concerts were advertised in the *HFP* almost from the beginning. Larry Norman and Dennis Agajanian headlined one of the earliest events in the Los Angeles area, a "Thanksgiving Feast of Music" in November 1969. A new band called the New Blue Earth joined them for a "Rock of Ages Folk Festival" in February 1970, and in the spirit of the times the admission was free and the posters and flyers reminded everyone to "bring a pillow." By the following summer, Capitol Records had released Norman's groundbreaking album "Upon this Rock," an LP hailed by some as the most original rock release since the Beatles' "Sgt. Pepper," but which 23-year-old Norman described simply as twelve love songs to Jesus.

By December 1970, we had booked the famed Hollywood Palladium theater for what we boldly advertised as the "first annual" Jesus People Festival of Music, hoping that the idea would catch on. What was planned as a three-hour Festival on a Sunday afternoon ran over five hours, and no one left, everyone was wanting more. At the very opening I asked all those who had come to the Festival for the sole purpose of inviting Jesus Christ into their life to stand.

People stood all across the Palladium. The music brought the young people in, but the Festivals were about Jesus and telling His story of salvation available through Him. When street preachers from the movement dropped in to a Festival, as they frequently did, we would always invite them up to the platform to speak.

The release of "Upon This Rock" dovetailed perfectly with the bright morning of the Jesus Movement, so it was natural that Christians would forever associate Norman and his music with the Jesus People revival. A seemingly fearless young man barely into his twenties when we met, he burst upon the scene and into our hearts with the bold proposition that Christian music was anemic and needed a transfusion.

Countless photos and film clips captured him playing and singing on stage at concerts and festivals. But I like to remember the Sunday afternoons when we would hear his Chevrolet Corvette screech to a halt outside the stage door on the Argyle Avenue side of the Palladium and Larry would burst through the door, struggling with his embroidered guitar strap and holding a Fender pick in his mouth, unscheduled, unannounced but ready to sing his heart out for the thousands of kids assembled in the theater who had played his records till the grooves wore out.

25

BOOM, WE'D START PREACHING

A flashback, if you will. Born and raised in Azusa, one of the many suburban "bedroom communities" that sprawl in all directions from Los Angeles, teenage musician Fred Caban was rapidly becoming a local guitar hero by the time he graduated from Azusa High School in 1968. His emerging style, an amalgam of psychedelic, blues and hard rock, was evocative of early Jimi Hendrix, or Eric Clapton's band Cream.

Fred and friends Jeff Newman and Major Cornell started a pickup band called The White Klapp with a couple of classmates; they played for dances and local clubs and won the school's 1968 Battle of the Bands. That summer, Caban and his bandmates decided to head down the coast in a Volkswagen microbus in search of venues at which to perform.

They parked the van at Huntington Beach, the first major surfing beach south of the Orange County line and a popular tourist destination. A former Teen Challenge drop-in center there had been renamed the Lightclub Outreach and reopened as a Christian coffeehouse for youth. In fact it was operated by David Berg and family, and was the base from which Berg would soon launch his controversial religious sect, the Children of God. But on that particular summer night, Fred Caban and his bandmates saw only a group of happy, eager young people that Fred would later describe as "totally immersed with the message of Christ." He was given a copy of the Gospel of John, which he said "for the first time answered some of the questions" that had been going through his mind.

Caban later recalled wandering down the beach and thinking, "if all this is true, I really want to know." He prayed, calling upon whoever was out there to reveal himself, a prayer strikingly similar to the one Lonnie Frisbee prayed in Tahquitz Canyon, and the response was just as immediate, and as dramatic. Caban said, "Jesus came to me and touched me on the shoulder. I actually saw Him, and He basically called me to follow Him."

He would later remember the encounter as "a very sobering moment for me, the conviction of the truth of His existence was so profound." He returned to the microbus and discovered that Jeff Newman had experienced a similar spiritual encounter. Together they went back to the Lightclub, shared what they each had experienced, and were both baptized that same night. In the morning the band drove back to Azusa.

Not long after his conversion experience in Huntington Beach, Caban formed a new band and named it Agape, one of several words in Koine Greek translated as "love," interpreted in a New Testament context to refer to God's love. Where previously their goal was to land a recording contract, the new band was motivated to preach the Gospel, and "began playing their old haunts with a new passion."

"We'd play one or two songs," Caban would later explain, "we'd jam, we'd blow them away, and then boom, we'd start preaching, and people would actually stick around and listen." In the beginning the band was unaware of the larger Jesus Movement that would soon ignite the entire west coast, but before long a ragtag little tribe of some 50 recent converts had loosely formed around the Agape band.

All or mostly teenagers from Azusa and surrounding towns in the San Gabriel valley, they responded eagerly to opportunities to promote the band's upcoming gigs at beaches, coffeehouses and the Los Angeles County Fair in nearby Pomona. When Caban and his bandmates organized some simple Bible studies, the teens, their numbers growing by word-of-mouth and the band's performances at local school assemblies, quickly got involved.

26

AFTER MIDNIGHT

By this time, the First Presbyterian Church of Hollywood had started a unique coffeehouse ministry, the Salt Company, modeled after the 1950s beatnik rendezvous in Greenwich Village. Launched in an aging apartment building to the rear of the church property, behind the gothic brick sanctuary that dominates the corner of Gower and Carlos, the coffeehouse would later move to a more suitable location across from Hollywood High School.

The church's pioneering college and youth pastor, Don Williams, led the new ministry, and it quickly became known locally as a performance venue for Christian solo musicians and bands, hosted by Lance Bowen, who also contributed his artistic talents to the *HFP*. Larry Norman became a frequent performer at the Salt Company when he moved to southern California, as well as Fred Caban's new band Agape.

Norman arranged to bring Caban, drummer Mike Jungkman and bassist John Peckhart to a local recording studio where they were introduced to record producer Martin Jones. Jones later offered to "comp" the band some free studio time with one minor catch — it had to be after midnight and before six in the morning. Agape used the late-night sessions to start tracking their debut album, "Gospel Hard Rock," which would be released on their own Mark label in 1971. The band released a second album a year later, titled "Victims of Tradition."

27

UNDER THE BIG AGAPE TENT

It was during the recording of "Gospel Hard Rock" that Caban met an Azusa Pacific student named Ron Turner through the Salt Company's Don Williams. Turner was studying to enter the ministry, and was serving as youth minister at Arcadia Community Church in the suburban foothills not far from Azusa. Turner invited Agape to perform at the church, and welcomed the band's growing troop of young converts to attend worship services.

Before long the informal group took on its own identity, and began meeting outdoors at Covina Park, a large, woodsy city park in an older residential neighborhood adjacent to Covina's Inter-Community Hospital. Turner, a formidable sight in a heavy Navy-style pea coat and full beard, began to take on more responsibility as Church in the Park's primary leader and teacher, and the unorthodox congregation grew to more than 500. On some Sundays, a dozen or more young Jesus People would be lined up waiting for their turn at the microphone to tell what Jesus was doing in their lives.

Turner soon added an innovative outdoor Bible study on Wednesday evenings, on the lawn at the Azusa Pacific campus. The study was structured with small group breakout sessions facilitated by a team of co-leaders, and over a period of several years covered "most of the essential books of the New Testament."

"We basically started on the lawn behind the library that they were building at the time," Ron Turner would later recall, "with about 35 kids in 1968. We moved around the campus to various lawns as we grew to about 300 over the years and Agape Church in the Park was between 500 and 700 on Sundays. The first Sunday, there were only twelve, and in three months it grew to about 500. They were pretty exciting days, seeing God's word touch hearts and lives."

Turner also organized a number of retreats held at Forest Home, a Christian camp and conference center founded by Sunday School pioneer Henrietta Mears of First Presbyterian Hollywood, the church that would later start the Salt Company and other groundbreaking ministries. Turner led the retreats with guest speakers including Dr. George Ladd, a professor of New Testament exegesis at Fuller Theological Seminary in Pasadena.

Caban's band continued to play venues across an ever-expanding swath of southern California, and was an integral part of Church in the Park. The group swarmed into the popular spring break destination of Palm Springs with a crew of teens from the Church in the Park congregation during Easter Week 1970. "Heads up Palm Springs," we announced in the *Hollywood Free Paper*, "here's how it's stacking up: Agape is invading!"

And invade they did, beginning with a concert at Salton Sea the Tuesday before Easter, a teen fair and concert on Wednesday, then a four-day series of concerts and other activities "under the big Agape tent" in Palm Springs. Events included a communion service on Good Friday and a sunrise service and baptism on Easter Sunday.

28

THIS CROSS IS MY FRIEND

Another flashback. Caravans of cars painted with peace symbols and flowers were parked haphazardly on the shoulder of the road in any available spot. Barefoot young women in ankle-length handmade granny dresses mingled with long-haired, bearded young men in jeans and handmade linen shirts, some without shirts, some wearing makeshift headbands fashioned from leafy ivy vines. Musicians played drums, flutes and tambourines as someone with an 8mm home movie camera wandered about shooting a blurry record of the day. Cannabis smoke mingled with sandalwood incense, and most were sailing on a dose of Orange Sunshine LSD from the Brotherhood of Eternal Love.

The scene was a summer "love-in" at Hollywood's rustic Griffith Park. A short-haired young man that Christianity Today would later describe as fresh-faced and hopelessly conservative ventured into the crowd in a suit and tie handing out religious tracts. He couldn't have looked more out of place. A southern farm boy from Greenville, Mississippi, he had grown up working on his father's cotton farm in northeast Louisiana, and on that day in Griffith Park he was a newly-minted graduate of a Bible college in the Deep South. "I was interested in going where the young people were gathering and sharing love," he explained, "and help them connect with the real Jesus."

The earnest young man reappeared the following March, now bearded with long hair, and rented a vacant building nextdoor to a topless go-go club on the Sunset Strip. He decorated the vacant space with colored lights and a large wooden cross on the wall, and posted a sign above the heavy wooden door: His Place. Arthur Blessitt was creating the first Jesus nightclub.

Arthur began to preach onstage at the famous Gazarri's rock-and-roll nightclub on the Strip where another earnest young man, Jim Morrison, fronted the house band, the Doors. "Jesus is your friend, not your enemy," Blessitt would tell the clubgoers. "You don't need pills, just drop a little Matthew, Mark, Luke and John." People began calling Blessitt the "Minister of Sunset Strip," and His Place soon had its own house band, the Eternal Rush.

He began doing midnight "soul sessions" at His Place, often leading drug addicts to literally flush their pills, marijuana and other drugs down the toilet in the club's tiny bathroom. At one point our friend Ron Bufton drew a marvelous cartoon of a new Christian happily flushing his stash of pills down the toilet, and this became the logo for "Set Free," our new column of testimonies from brothers and sisters who had overcome drugs, alcohol and other life problems through Jesus.

About two months after the first issue of the *Hollywood Free Paper* hit the street, Arthur took the 12-foot, 45-pound cross down from the wall of His Place, attached a small tricycle wheel, and set out to walk with it from Los Angeles to Washington, DC. "This wood is my friend," he would later explain. "You'd be amazed how much attention a man carrying a big wooden cross gets."

Eventually, His Place closed, and Arthur became a full-time pilgrim with his huge cross. He took the cross to war-torn Northern

Ireland, Spain, Morocco, Nicaragua, and the jungles of Panama through the Darien Gap. "I intend to keep going till God tells me to stop," he once declared. "My church and congregation are out there on the road."

29

ONE WAY -THE JESUS WAY

One of the major events of the holiday season in southern California is of course the Tournament of Roses, the seemingly endless parade of marching bands, equestrian riders and flower-decked floats in the Pasadena sun. The festivities actually begin the night before, as thousands upon thousands of tourists and locals line up along the parade route with sodas, junk food and blankets to brave the cold January night. For several years at the height of the Jesus Movement, we organized a large group of young Jesus People to invade the sidewalks of the parade route on New Year's Eve night with armloads of *HFP* newspapers.

For New Year's 1971, Billy Graham had been selected to be grand marshal of the parade, and when we heard that the City of Pasadena was expecting crowds of 200,000 or more along the parade route, we published a special New Year's edition of the *HFP* just for handing out on the parade route.

Perhaps one of the best accounts of that day was written by a friend of ours, historian Larry Eskridge from Wheaton College. He wrote about "an assorted band of street Christians handing out nearly 200,000 copies of the *Hollywood Free Paper*" in the early hours of New Year's day, and that "at some point, Graham began to notice that a number of young people were holding up placards ... and standing with raised index finger lifted upward shouting 'One way!' Suddenly, Graham remembered, 'we were made dramatically aware that a brand new spiritual awakening was on the way.'" Soon, "Graham was gesturing and shouting too: 'One way - the Jesus way!'"

We had sponsored a Jesus Festival at the First Baptist Church in Pasadena, and their fellowship hall served as a sort of 'staging area' where we organized to go out and witness and distribute *HFP*s by the thousands. The theme of the parade that year was "Happiness is...", and we had printed posters proclaiming "Happiness is JESUS!"

One of the young people who was there, who still works with me today, recalls that "at First Baptist Pasadena in that big fellowship room with the stone fireplace, we all had a communion service before we traveled to Pasadena to the Rose Parade where we were each given a bundle of *HFP*s to hand out to people spending the night on the parade route. Most of them were bored because the parade was still hours away, and they were happy to be given something interesting to read."

"I not only remember the young people with the signs, I was one of them," he writes. "My recollection years later is that two girls and I were holding up a large stenciled sign that (I think) said 'Jesus People', and we cheered and did 'one way' gestures when Billy passed by in the convertible. He pointed right at us, and then waved to us as he went by. And later that year I was thrilled to discover that Billy actually described that moment in his book. He really remembered us!"

30

SPIRITUAL REVOLUTION DAY

In late 1970 a young man from the Youth for Christ organization named Rich Weaver formed a committee called Students for a Spiritual Revolution, and began working with California state assemblyman Newton Russell (R-21st) to get February 13, 1971 declared "Spiritual Revolution Day" in Sacramento. Russell championed a bill through the state assembly, and governor Ronald Reagan signed a proclamation. The headline of our February 2, 1971 issue of the *HFP* proudly proclaimed the much-awaited news that "Calif Senate Proclaims Spiritual Revolution Day."

Thousands of Jesus People marched through the streets of Sacramento from O'Neil Field to a mass rally on the west steps of the state capitol, complete with music from the bands The New Scene and Mustard Seed, and speeches. A famous photograph of the march shows Larry Norman, Arthur Blessitt and Jack Sparks leading a throng of young people carrying signs that read "One Way - His Way" and "Jesus People Unite." At the rally following the march, student leaders presented their vision for spiritual revolution.

The Jesus People film "Son Worshippers" includes scenes from that rally, including Arthur Blessitt and Newton Russell speaking to the crowd. I appeared in an earlier scene of that film, singing and clapping with a group of young people, wearing my fringed leather vest that I was seldom without in those days.

Our coverage featured more than two full pages of photographs of the march and gathering. "The thousands of Jesus People who marched on California's state capitol held more than a belief in common," Larry Norman wrote in the *HFP*. "They have experienced results. Their personal prisons have been blown open. Their problems have begun to leave. They've experienced God-liberation."

31
SURF'S UP

Surfing is an important, exciting part of southern California culture, and our frequent ocean baptisms and beach evangelism had attracted the attention of local surfers. We decided to orient an entire issue of the *HFP* toward surfers and surfing.

"If a few drugs, a few girls, and a lot of surf is all there is to life," wrote surfer Cheer Critchlow of Cardiff-by-the-Sea, "then I was caught up in an absurd joke." Cheer found his way out of that absurd joke when he found the truth in Jesus. "A sincere person affects me stronger than any other," he wrote, "and Jesus was so fantastically sincere."

South Bay surfer Mike de Noune had achieved his dream of becoming a professional surfer for a major surfboard manufacturer, but discovered "the mystique that I thought was there wasn't, and they were as lost as I was. I gave my whole heart to surfing, and it never loved me back. It could never satisfy what I wanted inside, just to be peaceful and free." Mike found the peace and freedom he sought for in Jesus. "He gave me everything."

"Before I became a new creature in Christ," wrote surfer Margo Godfrey of La Jolla, "the framework and lifestyle through which I expressed myself and sought fulfillment of my needs was the sport of surfing." Starting at age 10, Margo found success in her sport, winning every major competition for female surfers and becoming a sponsored professional. Surfing was satisfying "while I was on the wave, but I felt empty and lost on those days when the surf was bad." After searching for meaning in yoga, meditation, health food and Eastern mysticism, Margo "realized there was a 'me' inside this body that needed to be released." She found that release in Jesus, along with the desire for "an intimate walk with Christ."

Mike de Noune and a number of other local surfers attended Bethel Tabernacle in north Redondo Beach near Los Angeles. It was a non-traditional church, with barefoot surfers tracking sand in and out of the sanctuary, and with the influx of Jesus People it became even more so. Founded shortly after World War II as an independent Pentecostal mission, Bethel had long ministered to those who found themselves living on the streets. A farmer from Woodruff, Kansas, named Lyle Steenis and his wife Doris started the small church in 1948, and under their leadership it grew to a congregation of 300, mostly white middle-class suburbanites.

In 1969, a sudden influx of young people, both surfers and Jesus People, almost turned the tiny church upside-down. "They brought their friends," columnist Linda Riley would later write in *Christianity Today*, "and soon the services overflowed with barefoot, long-haired types wearing love beads." The new arrivals, Riley relates, "wanted to pray till all hours of the night. They moved in together for fellowship till their homes looked like communes." The older traditional members began to wonder if Bethel was becoming "a hippie church [or] a cult."

Steenis recruited Breck Stevens, a handsome refugee from the drug culture with a magnetic personality, to help the church establish a better rapport with the young surfers, Jesus freaks and hippies that were increasingly making Bethel their offbeat church home. Stevens soon found himself fulfilling a similar function at Bethel that Lonnie Frisbee was at Calvary Chapel of Costa Mesa. Both churches found themselves being radicalized and transformed — not by the hippies, but by the Holy Spirit — and caught up in a literal Jesus revolution.

32

THY BROTHER'S HOUSE

Another flashback. It was the summer of 1970. Stacks of empty berry cartons marked rain-soaked acres of strawberries along State College Drive in Fullerton as migrant farmworkers tumbled from a retired school bus to pick berries in the early morning fog. A stone's throw away, a fledgling public university was in the throes of expansion to fill its sprawling campus, built on 236 acres of former citrus groves planted by a descendant of the real Johnny Appleseed.

Southern California's Orange County was changing fast, and as the pale morning sun silhouetted oak trees and housetops against the horizon of misty hills to the east, the sleepy agricultural settlement of Fullerton was evolving from its rural beginnings in Valencia oranges and row crops to a suburban community of tract homes surrounding its namesake college.

Middle-school teacher Frank Huston and his wife Martha had recently returned to the area from a trip to San Francisco, and along the way they had visited several of the early "house ministries" that would soon become known as Jesus houses. It was during this road trip up the coast that the Hustons became aware of the still nascent Jesus People movement and saw for themselves the Spirit "working among the young people."

Upon their return, they attended beach baptisms at Corona del Mar, visited Chuck Smith's thriving Calvary Chapel in Costa Mesa, and "rejoiced to see what God was doing." Soon, the Hustons felt led to start a house ministry like the ones they had seen along the coast, and with two other couples, Bill and Sharon Trimper and Gus and Peggy McAuley, they opened Thy Brother's House on Harbor Boulevard in Fullerton near the university.

The concept of Thy Brother's House was unique, serving as a central Bible study and mini-concert venue for other Jesus houses in northeast Orange County that lacked facilities for large gatherings. Soon there were scores of young people coming to the house for concerts, evangelistic outreaches and extended prayer meetings that "convinced us that God was indeed doing something special." It was during this period that the Hustons met Ron Turner and Fred Caban of Agape, witnessed the early beginnings of Chuck Girard and Jay Truax's band Love Song, hosted an Earth Harvest concert that featured Larry Norman and Randy Stonehill, and gained a new vision of the rapidly expanding Jesus People movement. During that exciting period, Frank would later say, "We became more exposed to what God was doing all over the region."

By the spring of 1971, in addition to those living at Thy Brother's House, a number of young people were living with the Hustons in their three-bedroom home in Fullerton. As they began to look for a larger home to accommodate the growing tribe, Frank and Martha were approached by several young people from the San Gabriel valley to start a ministry similar to Thy Brother's House in their area.

33

GREEN PASTURES

The Hustons' search led them to Pomona, a suburb at the southeast corner of the San Gabriel valley just over the Puente Hills from Fullerton. Once a stable community with a thriving downtown and local industries including aerospace giant General Dynamics and three paper mills, by the early 1970s Pomona was wrestling with a sluggish economy and growing racial tension.

The two-story white clapboard house the Hustons found on Sheridan Avenue in Pomona was a classic New England farmhouse, built during the area's agricultural heyday in 1882 when Pomona was the hub of the local citrus industry. Stately in its construction with a large columned porch and bay windows, the house stood at the center of a two-acre parcel with a smaller tree-shaded cottage to the rear. Several large bedrooms could easily be outfitted with dorm-style bunk beds, Frank Huston figured, and the back cottage would be ideal for a music venue to hold mini-concerts. The Lord provided the means, and the new Jesus house soon opened with the name Green Pastures.

The house was in a quiet, older residential neighborhood, so the soon-to-be houseparents worried about complaints from neighbors about noise, parking, the volume level of live music, and a never-ending stream of hippies and other youth coming and going at all hours. They needn't have worried. Green Pastures never received one complaint from neighbors or police.

By late 1971, some 21 Jesus People were living in the Green Pastures house, a young couple was living in an old Chevrolet delivery van, and a college student, Ken Irons, was camping in an Indian teepee in the backyard, but still none of the neighbors complained. Ken had been baptized by Chuck Smith at one of the beach baptisms at Corona del Mar, and was attending California State Polytechnic University in Pomona, better known as Cal Poly. He helped Frank build more bunk beds, enclosed the porch so it could be used as an eating area, and converted the smaller back house into an expanded bunkroom.

The Green Pastures community was one of several Jesus People groups that traveled to the Sierra Nevada mountains of central California in the spring of 1972. The groups spent a week hiking from the subalpine meadows of the meandering Tuolumne River into a pine-studded valley carved out of glacial granite by the swift waters of the mighty Merced River almost before time began. The Indians called it Yosemite. Frank Huston, Ken Irons and others from the Pomona house joined with other Jesus People for an unforgettable experience. Irons later recalled "the clean air, bright sunshine, frosty mornings and a few rainy days. What a rush that was. To be able to worship in that beautiful mountain setting beneath the brightly starlit sky at night was fantastic. Singing and worshipping around the stuttering and snapping fire was magical."

AFTERWORD

This book chronicles only the early West Coast beginnings of a movement that continued for several more years and would eventually spread to every state of the Union and on to Canada, Scandinavia, Mexico, the Philippines, and some say even further.

It would be impossible to chronicle such a widespread and varied movement in its entirety. In particular the many artists, albums and songs that made up the music of the movement have been described and catalogued much better elsewhere than we can here.

Perhaps the most important legacy of the movement was its return to the simple Gospel and the New Testament prototype of Christianity, centered in the life and teachings of Jesus and demanding a personal relationship with Him.

Today, the Jesus People Movement lives on in the hearts and minds of every brother and sister who remembers those times and is still following Jesus.

"Fear not, little flock, for it is your Father's good pleasure to give you the kingdom." - Luke 12:32, ASV

Made in the USA
Lexington, KY
09 October 2016